ESCAPING THE CHAINS OF GRIEF

Live Life with Purpose On Purpose

Kimberly Smith Dauterive, M.D.

Copyright © 2024

All Rights Reserved

No part of this book may be reproduced or transmitted in any form or by any means, electronic or mechanical, including photocopying, recording, or by any information storage and retrieval system without the written permission of the author, except where permitted by law.

SCAN THE QR CODE

AND COMPLETE THE FORM FOR MORE
GREAT RESOURCES & A FREE EXCERPT FROM
MY EBOOK *FROM BURNOUT TO BLISS*

Follow Me @ DoctorKSD_Evolved

This book is dedicated to Phillip "Poppa" Dauterive III, my Poppa Bear. I'm forever grateful to God for allowing me to be your mother. Though I wish I could have spent forever with you here on this earth, I am grateful for the nine years, ten months, and 10 days we had together. They were some of the most magnificent days of my life.

Poppa was an old man in a little boy's body. He had wisdom beyond his years, unconditional love for everyone he met, a knack for lifting your spirits when you were down, and the ability to inspire you to be better and do better. He made our family stronger and has left a lasting impression on so many lives that four years following his departure to Paradise, I am still hearing stories of how he made a remarkable impact on somebody's life, both young and old.

Poppa, I didn't think I would survive your death, but you've proven that even from Heaven, you continue to uplift and empower. Thank you for helping me find my voice and giving me the courage to stretch myself and impact lives, not just in my immediate environment and communities, but across the world with this book, my online coaching program, and my speaking career. I am forever grateful for you! My heart will never be the same because your physical absence has left a void that nothing can replace but better to have spent nine years, 10 months, and 10 days with you than to never have had you at all. I love you always baby boy, and I can't wait to see you again in Paradise one day.

Love, Mom

Table of Contents

Chapter One: The Deception of Grief 1

Chapter Two: The Revelation 6

    Reflections: 10

Chapter Three: Secret #1 The Emotional Roller Coaster 12

    Reflections: 24

Chapter Four: Secret #2 The Purge 26

    Reflections: 33

Chapter Five: Secret #3 Traditions We Shouldn't Inherit 36

    Reflections: 45

Chapter Six: Secret #4 Jesus Grieved 47

    Reflections: 54

Chapter Seven: Secret #5 It is NOT Good for Grievers to Grieve Alone 58

    Reflections: 70

Chapter Eight: Secret #6 Time Is Not a Healer of a Broken Heart 73

    Reflections: 80

Chapter Nine: SECRET #7 Moving Forward Doesn't Mean Forgetting Your Loved One 83

    Reflections: 93

Chapter Ten: Live Life With Purpose On Purpose 95

Reflections:	106
Acknowledgments	110
About the Author	114

Chapter One: The Deception of Grief

Grief is normal and natural, but you wouldn't think so based on how society handles grief or, more specifically, how society treats grievers. The reality is that grief is a horrible feeling that every single person on this earth will inevitably experience. What's even worse, we will all experience the joy-draining jabs of grief more than once in our lifetime. This is what makes the fact that society treats grief as though it's a disease or a shameful act even worse because everyone knows what grief feels like yet still will judge grievers as though they don't.

There are so many reasons why people grieve. Grief rears its ugly head when people lose anything they hold precious and dear in their hearts. We have been wrongly raised to look at the death of a loved one as the only cause of grief. And that is a huge part of the problem. Unfortunately, there are many other things we deem priceless and valuable that can be ripped away

Escaping the Chains of Grief

from us, setting off the cascade of emotional labor pains that give birth to grief.

We can all agree that the loss of a loved one is at the top of the list when we think of the causes of grief, but let us not belittle other important things like the loss of a pet, the loss of a business, being trapped in a loveless marriage, the loss of a home, the loss of finances, divorce, the loss of a friendship, the loss of innocence, betrayal, the loss of trust, moving to a new neighborhood away from familiar faces, leaving the security of your home after graduating and going off to college, being promoted and leaving your friends behind or any of the other numerous things which can cause a change in the normalcy of one's life that leads to the loss of what was once considered special and valuable. And yes, grief even shows up in situations where others may feel you should be grateful and elated because what many don't or rather won't understand, having never been in those situations, is that regardless of the amount of money you make or the number of materialist things you may have if you lose your freedom, your voice, or especially your peace of mind, no amount of money or things will prevent the painful chains of grief from locking onto your soul and draining you of every ounce of hope, happiness, and joy you may have.

Again, no one will escape being caught by the chains of grief at least once, yet many still refuse to understand and acknowledge the magnitude of the power grief can hold over someone. I mean, you would swear that grievers are the villains of society the way they are treated. Some people go out of their way to avoid grievers. Some will chastise grievers for grieving too long. Some will quickly tell tearful grievers to excuse themselves to another room to "go and collect" themselves away from the public. And some are even inconsiderate enough to tell grievers they need to move on as though dismissing the loss is that simple a matter.

Grievers from generation to generation have been unfairly treated this way. Why do you think that is?

Personally, I believe it's because people, in general, have a problem dealing with the negative emotions they feel. We live in a society where a person will be shunned, judged, and gossiped about when they don't align with what society has deemed as good and acceptable. Anyone who dares to color outside of the lines drawn by society becomes disliked and,

Escaping the Chains of Grief

therefore, the recipient of the hateful words and opinions of society. And who do you know that wants to be on the receiving end of that type of assault? So, for most, it's easier to stay within those lines even when that means hiding their real emotions and becoming an imposter in their own lives. But that's not the end of it. Because so many are afraid to stand up to society's ideals, they are equally and maybe even unknowingly opposed to anyone who has the courage to act exactly how they feel. In turn, when a griever has the audacity to be sad and tearful, the cowardly imposters who've managed to hide their pain behind laughter and smiles judge them.

So, to avoid the assault, grievers hide their painful emotions. And the more those emotions try to push themselves to the surface and reveal themselves, the further down they get pushed. Regardless of whether those emotions are buried by the coward who doesn't want to go against society or by the fearful one who doesn't want to be judged by society, the absence of properly dealing with grief becomes a way of life that gets passed down from generation to generation and instead of proper grief management being one of the many important things we teach our children, we end up teaching them that grief is bad and should not be expressed and create an army of children with unexpressed emotions who are molded into uncaring, unsympathetic adults whose relationships are all affected by those same unexpressed emotions that they worked so hard to bury. And that negatively affects so many areas of their lives.

The problem is that all those unspoken emotions stay buried for so long that they become deeply rooted within the soul and eventually control a person's reaction to every aspect of their life. And grief that is not properly dealt with will ultimately lead to the loss of a person's dreams, hope, and purpose. Those unspoken emotions are the very emotions that cause one to simply exist from day to day rather than live and enjoy life. They are ultimately the crafty thief that robs us of our lives.

Chapter Two: The Revelation

When my 9-year-old son died, I thought I would never recover. I mean, how could I? It was just so final. There was no turning back. There was no pressing the rewind button so that I could go and change things. There was nothing that I could do that would reverse the fact that a distracted driver drove into their lane and hit the car my husband and baby boy were in forever, taking my precious son away from me. Absolutely, nothing could change that! So, how could I ever even imagine living a life of purpose again when I could barely get out of bed to go to the bathroom? But I kept praying and asking God for the strength to get me through another second, then another minute, then another hour, then another day.

And let's get something straight: I was not praying for me or my own wellbeing. I was praying that prayer because I had an injured husband who survived but still needed me in a major way, and I had other children who still depended on me for strength and encouragement. But how could I give them strength and encouragement when I had none to give? Yeah, I wasn't praying that prayer for me just to get stronger. I was praying that prayer because of the love I have for my family and my desire that they survive and thrive despite the painful and difficult hand we were dealt.

But something wonderful happened to me as I prayed and prayed throughout the day every day. The more I bared my soul to God, the more I expressed those horrible, shattering, and excruciating emotions I had inside, and the more I purged and flushed out all those horrid emotions that were trying desperately to take root within my soul. As I continued to pray, the Lord started digging up those terrible emotional roots, pulling up those nasty emotional weeds, and destroying all evidence of negativity, defeat, and loss of hope that tried to overtake my very being. It was then that I realized why people are so easily bound and overtaken by grief… they are too afraid to express those painful emotions because they have never been taught that to face them and express them is the key to being free of them.

The more I expressed my emotions, the stronger I felt and the less I cared about how society felt about my expression of my grieving the loss of my son. If I felt like crying in the middle of the day while sitting in the room with one of my patients, I did. If I felt like being sad during a get-together with my friends or colleagues, I did. You see, I came to the life-changing realization that I am not responsible for how anyone else feels about anything, especially about my grief. The moment I stopped caring about what other people thought who had never experienced what I was experiencing, I was freed from the jaws of grief, and my life was given back to me.

Now, don't get me wrong, I still miss my son. Oh, how I miss him so much! And I've come to grips with the fact that every single morning when I wake up, and I'm hit with the reality that he is really gone from this physical world forever, I will be sad. But just because I'm sad doesn't mean that grief has the right to take away everything else that's good and wonderful from my life. And neither should you allow grief to do that to you.

Because you see, I still have a lot to live for: my husband, my children, my future grandchildren, and my purpose... and so do you! And I want to share the secrets to escaping and help you get beyond that place where grief has taken root, and those unexpressed emotions have started invading every fiber of your soul. Yes, I want for you the freedom from the prison of grief that I've found. I want us to dig deep and uproot the grief weeds, pull them out, and destroy them forever so that we can live a life that is again filled with hope and dreams. Let me help you turn your pain into purpose.

Reflections:

What are some of your life experiences that have caused you to grieve (Death of loved ones, lost relationships, marriage, divorce, etc.)?

What emotions has grief caused to invade your mind, heart, and soul against your will?

Do you feel comfortable expressing your emotions caused by grief in front of others? If not, explain why you don't.

Are you ready to escape the hold that grief has had on you?

Chapter Three: Secret #1 The Emotional Roller Coaster

If you hang around the elderly long enough, you'll eventually hear this phrase, "The only thing I have to do is pay taxes and die." And guess what? They are one hundred percent correct, at least about the dying part, anyway. Death is not something that we can escape. The Bible tells us that our days are numbered. Therefore, as much as we may not want to have to deal with death, the truth is we are not given a choice in the matter. It is unavoidable. And though we all know that death is inevitable, isn't it strange that we are still never prepared when death finally does come knocking at our door? Even when it comes to our elderly parents and grandparents, death still feels like a thief robbing us of our loved ones. Yes, even those who are old and frail and have lived a long, good life. And what's just as bad is that we are fully at a disadvantage when it comes to dealing with the emotional roller coaster that we are forcefully thrust onto when it actually happens.

Poppa's death caused a huge gaping wound to form right in the center of my heart that, four years later, is still very present. To be perfectly honest, I cannot imagine how it will ever heal when I know every morning, I must wake up to the horrible reality that Poppa, my sweet baby boy, is truly gone. You see, I left for work on the morning of August 27, 2019, after giving Poppa a kiss and a hug, fully expecting to see him when I returned home later that evening. But that just didn't happen because the split-second, tragically irresponsible decision of a distracted driver unfairly ripped him from my life and my family's forever. I was broken. No! I was shattered into a million pieces, and nothing could have prepared me for the level of brokenness with feelings of dismay, despair, and emptiness that I would feel upon learning of his death.

Just thinking about it now causes all of those raw and bitter emotions I felt on that awful day to come rushing back into every fiber of my body, drawing tears to my eyes. There was no way I could have fortified myself enough and nothing that I could have done to be properly prepared for the atrocious and sickening emotions that attacked my soul. In the blink of an eye, I lost the physical connection I had to my baby boy, my son-shine, my peacemaker, my joy, the glue that brought our blended family together. Just like that! No rewind. No playback. No do-over. Just gone! It all just still seems so surreal and, honestly, unbelievable that death is so final.

I cannot even remember the number of times I have had to deal with death as a physician, nor the number of families I've had to break the horrible news to and counsel. And in the 23 years I've been practicing, I never recalled death feeling so final. Final! There is no going back. There is no pressing rewind. There is no do-over. That's it? How could that be it? Just like that, my sweetheart of a son was gone. And just like that, the happy, joy-filled, and serene state of my heart was forever broken and scarred in a way that it would never be whole again.

The multitude of emotions that bombarded me all at once was unbelievable. Imagine having all the different colors of paint pallets thrown at your immaculate white outfit all at once. The mess that you can imagine pretty much sums up the mess of emotions that were running wild throughout my heart and soul. I mean, I went from angry to sad to enraged to deeply hurt to feeling some semblance of peace because "God doesn't make mistakes" to livid about how horribly unfair it was to feeling betrayed to defeated, and then to shattered and broken. But the strongest emotion of them all was the agonizing, excruciating pain that seemed to pierce my soul, separating it from my spirit, touching every single cell in my body mercilessly, leaving me feeling like a shell of the person I was a mere 5 minutes or so before I realized my baby boy was gone from this earth forever.

I had never in my life felt that type of gut-wrenching pain before. I remember wondering, "Lord, how do people survive this? How CAN they survive this?" I couldn't fathom getting through the day, let alone getting through a week, a month, or a year. It just hurt too much! But I feel my omniscient God orchestrated His plan so perfectly as He always does to undoubtedly ensure my survival through it all. Though I felt like giving up and though I felt too weak to even want to do anything for myself, I could not give up and throw in the towel because I had a loving husband who needed me and wonderful children who did as well. Because I loved them just as much as I loved Poppa, God knew my natural instinct would be to push beyond the pain and weakness I was feeling to make sure that I was able to be there for them. And I did what I had to do to show up in whatever capacity they needed me to show up for them every time. But anything that related to just me, I did not have the strength nor the desire to make myself do it.

I even remember how horrified I felt one night while crying out to God for comfort when I thought of the many people, especially parents, I had counseled in the past after they suffered the loss of a loved one and thought to myself, "My God, I had no idea they were feeling this broken, lost and shattered!" Nothing could have prepared me for the 18-wheeler carrying 33 tons of emotional distress that hit me at the sound of my name being said in such a way that I knew my baby was gone as the nurse and state trooper walked me through the emergency room to the place where my Poppa lay. The realization stole my strength. I still hear my own words screaming out, "It's not fair! It's not fair!" To know that every parent who has lost a child has felt that type of agonizing, soul-snatching pain is such a horrible thing, and every time I learn of another parent losing their child, I am catapulted back to that day and those feelings and pray that God will help them get through those initial weeks that are sure to bring them to the brink of insanity.

The first few months after losing Poppa, it was hard to see anything but darkness and gloom all around me. Then, when a whole year later, I found myself just as sad and depressed as I was on that tragic day. I realized I was not healing at all. Not even a little bit. I mean, I would have moments when I felt like I was getting stronger and would feel hopeful that I was finally moving over the hump of grief, but they were only fleeting. Just as quickly as the hopefulness dared to penetrate my heart, in the bat of an eye, there grief was again taunting me and promising never to leave my side. Nothing I did would make the pain go away and stay away. I felt defeated and could not imagine that anything ever would make it disappear forever.

But wait! Why was this happening? I was so confused! This was not my first encounter with death. My mother had died in March of the same year Poppa was born. I did not feel any of these chaotic and disruptive emotions when she died. None of this was making any sense at all. I just couldn't shake the emotional turmoil that continued to haunt my soul each day following Poppa's death, and I did not understand why. I mean, in my profession as a physician, I deal with death all the time. I have had to deliver the awful news to families. I have had to walk families through the grieving process. Heck, I was not the first to lose a loved one, and I definitely was not the first mother to lose a child. This made no sense to me. And as a Christian, I had no doubt that Poppa was in Heaven. So why couldn't I get past this?! Surely, this was not my fate for the rest of my existence here on earth, to live in emotional distress and grief, void of life and purpose. Right? I was starting to lose all hope until I stumbled across secret number one.

The first secret to escaping the chains of grief is acknowledging that the loss of your significant someone or something (your great loss) has opened Pandora's box of emotions that has been given the green light to run rampant in the depths of your soul where it wreaks havoc destroying all semblance of peace and joy and all matters of hope for the future. It robs you of your desire to live a life of purpose and literally forces you onto the scariest and most complex emotional roller coaster that you will ever ride. A ride, I might add, that you do not even have the option to get off of because it is never-ending.

The first few years after Poppa died, I was torpedoed with a myriad of emotions that vacillated from sadness to anger to despair to frustration to gloom and finally to peace.

Deceivingly, though, it was only a false sense of peace because while it seemed like the chaotic disruption within my soul was coming to a progressive halt, the reality was that the emotional roller coaster ride was not slowing down at all but simply gearing up to gain momentum to start all over again. That false sense of peace was the worst because it lured me into believing that I was finally "healing," only to blindside me with a relentless onslaught of pain and brokenness that rivaled the day of the crash.

This emotional roller coaster ride went a little something like this…

The emotional roller coaster would slowly make its way up to the very top of the tracks, causing feelings of happiness, excitement, and even hopefulness at the possibility of healing, being better, and getting stronger. Then suddenly and surprisingly, it would plummet towards the ground, symbolic of the turbulent grief that would sneak up on me out of the blue, turning my world upside down with such great force that it would cause a scream to escape from my lips while vicious summersaults threatened to evacuate all the contents of my stomach. And just when I would think I could take it no more, the blessing of a small reprieve would come along as everything would level off, ushering in a much-needed period of calm. But that would be short-lived because soon I would find myself being flipped and thrown around like a rag doll in a dog's mouth as I would be taken through a series of sharp curves left, right, and, oh my Lord, even upside-down, causing feelings of panic, depression, and despair to emerge. And suddenly, with my hands gripping tightly, going numb from the death hold I had on the supposed security bar, everything would come to a screeching pause. The calm would envelop me, allowing peace to flow inside uninhibited and welcomed, followed by movement at a snail's crawl, generating a feeling of false hope that healing was surely near. Excitement would join in as more peace and stability would be ushered in, and I would, with suspicious hesitation, decrease my grip on the bars and would slowly breathe easier as I would be taken back up to the top of the tracks where hope resides not recognizing the plummet was soon to come again.

This terrifying ride ran on repeat for about a year and a half. Have you ever been in a place in your life where you felt helpless and hopeless because you had no control over your emotional state from one minute to the next? Well, that is exactly where I was, except, I found myself in that place while still trying to force myself to be a wife, mother, friend, and physician, and that was by far one of the most difficult things I have ever had to do and one of the most defeated feelings I have ever had to experience. It was the only time in my life that I literally had to consistently talk myself out of just giving up.

It was then that I realized that the ride itself was worse because of my own opposition. You see, every time I was surprised with a new, sudden, and scary maneuver I was not prepared for that caught me off guard and made my heart beat faster, tears come to my eyes, and that brought on feelings of hopelessness and defeat, I would try to fight it because naturally, I did not want to go through any of that pain or fear. But it is when you fight the natural flow of things that damage is more likely to happen. In all matters of life, when you go with the current instead of fighting the current, you are more likely to survive and come out less damaged on the other side. There was light at the end of the tunnel with the realization that if I would just put my hands up, go with the flow of the ride, and simply ride the curves of the roller coaster whichever way it turned as it was going through its different maneuvers, I did not feel half as bad as when I went against the normal flow of the ride. Simply putting my hands in the air and riding the wave of the emotion allowed me to decrease the pain I was feeling by a huge percentage, and though I still felt sad and though it still made me cry, the tormenting pain that threatened to tear me to pieces was no longer as threatening. Going with the flow took away the sting and decreased the power it had over me.

So, I learned to ride the wave willingly and not to be ashamed to admit I was on that terrible emotional roller coaster. I no longer fought the feeling. If certain memories or sounds or smells and especially certain songs brought back fond, wonderful memories of my baby boy that ultimately led to feelings of hurt and disappointment at him not being here with me, I would just go with the wave and allow the emotion to have its way and have its time. I did not try to hold back my tears. I did not try to fight the feelings of sadness and grief. And I did not try to pretend like I was feeling good when I was feeling everything but good. Whenever I allowed the emotion to have its way, it shortened the time that emotion could wreak havoc in my soul.

So, although I am still riding that emotional roller coaster, it is not half as scary or traumatic as it initially was. And more importantly, it does not have the control over my emotions that it initially had. You see, I realized that as long as I put my arms up in the air and ride the wave of whatever emotion is showing up on any given day, I stay in control of my mental well-being and prevent those vile emotions from overpowering me and taking from me pieces of my joy and my hope as significantly as they once were able to do.

Reflections:

What does your emotional roller coaster look like? What are the different emotions that your emotional roller coaster takes you through?

Kimberly Smith Dauterive

Do you suffer through the emotional roller coaster ride alone, or do you grab hold of a lifeline to help you through it?

Chapter Four: Secret #2 The Purge

With the emotional storms having a field day in my head, heart, and soul, I got to the point where I just couldn't take it anymore. I had tried so hard to keep it together, not for myself but for my family. My husband was still counting on me because he was injured. Every day, he needed almost total assistance from me for at least the first two months following his hospitalization because he was so battered and bruised from the crash that he could not take care of all of his needs by himself. In addition to the physical assistance he needed, he also needed emotional support, having lost his youngest son, the son he prayed for God to send and the one with whom he spent almost every moment of his time. My daughter needed me because it was her senior year in high school, and my genius 4.0 student who had lost her little brother no longer wanted to spread her wings and fly off to New York for college but wanted to stay close to keep an eye on me. I knew that if I wanted her to have any chance at reaching her full potential and to take advantage of every opportunity available to her at the time, I could not let her throw her senior year away, even if her baby brother, her best friend, was gone. My oldest son still needed me, too, because he was thousands of miles away as a military man stationed abroad, contemplating transferring back to the States to be near me. Still, I knew his future success was dependent upon him staying there, where he was moving up the ranks at speeds unheard of before. So, I did what any real, virtuous wife and mother would do: I held on for dear life and did what I had to do to ensure the stability and well-being of my family for as long as I could. Unfortunately, the burden of grief was so heavy and so powerful, I was progressively losing the battle dreadfully.

I fought, though! I fought until I had no more fight in me. But the quilt of grief kept getting heavier, and I started to feel downright defeated. And for the first time in my life, I was ready to throw in the towel and give up. That in and of itself was horrifying because I have never given up on anything I set my mind to accomplish ever in my life. But I had never dealt with grief like this before, and I could not bear the pain any longer. So, I let go of the last ounce of strength I had left in me that had been holding everything together, and I cried. I mean, I really cried! Now, I am not talking about a nice little dainty, girly type of cry. I mean the kind of cry that came from the deepest, darkest, hidden recesses of my soul. The kind of cry that robbed me of my ability to stand upright. The kind of cry that made me scream and holler and have a proper temper tantrum right there on my bedroom floor. I cried about how unfair it was that my baby boy was taken from me! I cried about how unfair it was that I seemed to be the one always losing someone or something despite all that I would give of my time, my treasure, and myself freely each and every day to everyone and anyone who needed it. I cried about how tired I was having always to be the strong person for everyone in my life. I cried about not getting to see my baby boy graduate from the lower school, middle school, high school, or college. I cried about never seeing him dance again and never hearing his rambunctious laughter over all the house. I cried about never being able to do a TikTok with him because we never got around to doing one together. I even cried about him never making it to the NFL draft because it was spoken over his life by almost every sports fan who met him, even in his infancy. From birth, he was always above the 90th percentile rank for his age. He was born a whole three weeks earlier than his due date but still weighed in at a whopping 8lbs 3oz, and at the time of his leaving for Paradise at nine years old, he was almost as tall as me… 9.5-10 sized shoe in men, wore men's 36 in jeans and medium in shirts, stood tall at 5'0" and weighed 160lbs. Surely, my baby boy was going to be an NFL football player! And we had already fantasized about how we would all be there smiling on TV, proud of him, and of course, he would have to thank his mother first for all the love and nurturing he received ☺. I cried about all the things that I would never get to experience with the little boy who brought so much joy, laughter and love to our lives. I cried about how unfair it felt when I had done everything in my power to keep him as safe as I possibly could. Lord, did I cry! And that cry allowed me to "PURGE" all those nasty, unspoken emotions that I had locked away in my inner being, too afraid to think or speak of them for fear of coming across as selfish or crazy. I cried every tear that I could muster up in that moment until I could not cry anymore. And when I was spent and had shed my last tear, I finally picked myself up off the floor to go and wash my face and noticed that something miraculous seemed to have happened. I felt lighter!

But hold on… That could not be right, though. I had given up. I was just rolling on the floor, crying like a maniac, resolved that I would not survive Poppa's absence. This had to be a real mental breakdown I was going through. No way did I feel better. It just did not make any sense that I could feel lighter. Initially, I was afraid to ponder too hard and too long about the matter for fear I was dreaming and the heavy quilt of grief would drop down on me again from out of the blue. But sure enough, as time went on and I kept reassessing my state of mind from moment to moment, I realized that I truly did feel lighter than I had felt since that horrible crash took my Poppa away from me. Somehow, that "purge" removed the heavy load of grief I had been forced to carry around on my shoulders since August 27, 2019. I had discovered the second secret to escaping the jaws of grief.

This was absolutely a miracle! And that's when it hit me. I had the most amazing revelation! Total and one hundred percent transparent expression of my emotions was the key to being stronger, renewing my hope, and being able to live with purpose again. It was like the blinders had suddenly been removed from my eyes. I could see that releasing those horrific emotions that were building up inside of me was the key to being free of them. It was the key to feeling better and having hope. It was the key to waking up in the morning and getting out of bed. It was the key to trying to live a life with purpose again. But why was I even hiding my emotions in the first place, and why had I been hiding them for so long? I mean, I do have a right to cry and feel frustrated, angry, and hurt; however, I feel from one minute to the next. That was my baby boy who was taken from me! That was my heart shattered into a million pieces! That was my soul crushed, leaving me feeling worn and defeated! So, it's my right to feel however I feel and to be able to express how I feel freely without worrying about what others are going to say or think about it. Because the truth of the matter is this: Poppa was my child. I held him in my womb for nine months. I nurtured him and loved him like only a mother can love their child. And no one will ever make me feel as though I do not have a right to the many emotions that run through my soul every single day because of not being physically connected to my son!

Never again will I bury those emotions brought on by grief because I also realized that every time I "purged," I felt better. Now, do not get the wrong idea. Those emotions eventually build up again. But every time they build up again and I get to the point of feeling that disgusting, overwhelming grief, it is at that moment that I recognize it is time to "purge" again. And every time I "purge" I always come out on the other side feeling lighter, stronger, and more hopeful. Soon, I realized that what started to happen was every time I "purged," the length of time between "purges" started getting farther and farther apart. Initially, my "purge" occurred every day. That slowly changed to every other day. Then, soon after that, it changed to once or twice a week. Shortly after that, it changed to once or twice a month. Now I "purge" at least once every quarter, and even though I wake up with sadness every morning, the fact that I am no longer burying my emotions but in a healthy manner, I am "purging" when I need to do so has allowed me to live life with purpose on purpose as I deserve to live. And you deserve to live the same kind of life with purpose on purpose as well.

Kimberly Smith Dauterive

Reflections:

Does the thought of the "purge" cause feelings of relief or feelings of anxiety? If anxiety, why?

Escaping the Chains of Grief

Are there emotions that you have been too afraid to admit because you fear how they make you look to yourself and others?

How often do you "purge"?

If the cause of your grief occurred more than two years ago and you are still "purging" often, think about the emotions you may not be willing to admit to yourself that you are feeling inside and admit them now. Freedom can only come with you being honest with yourself.

Chapter Five: Secret #3 Traditions We Shouldn't Inherit

Tradition plays such a huge role in how we live, where we live, what college we choose, who we marry, and even how we raise our children. Tradition has been the cornerstone for how families build their legacy and ensure the safety, happiness, and prosperity of their bloodlines. In so many ways, tradition has been responsible for how and why businesses thrive, teams win, and people soar. Tradition is acceptable in so many instances as it has been proven to work. However, there is at least one place where tradition has no business having an influence, and that is when it is related to how people grieve. Tradition has no place inserting itself into the lives of grievers.

Passed down from generation to generation are dump trucks full of incorrect statements and practices concerning grief that have been proven to harm instead of help and hinder instead of liberate. These traditions of grief keep grievers from being able to appropriately and effectively express their emotions, which ultimately causes an internal grave to form where those emotions are buried, ultimately preventing the griever from being able to move on and reach their full potential. These emotions are buried, and instead of dying, they take root and become intricately woven within the depths of our souls until they take over and control our state of being from day to day. And that got me thinking. Why would we want our painful emotions to become rooted and grounded and gain access to control our souls, and just as importantly, why do people avoid expressing their emotions, especially when it comes to grieving the loss of someone or something significant in their lives (their great loss?)

Pondering this question, I came to the sad revelation that I had discovered the third secret to escaping the jaws of grief. Tradition should not be allowed to dictate how we grieve. Tradition allows grief to grow deep roots within our souls, overtaking our ability to thrive. It all goes back to lessons handed down to us from generation to generation concerning how we handle our emotions. We were taught to always keep our emotions in check. Regardless of whether we were mad at our house, at the store, at a festival, or in the church, staying in control of our emotions has always been a mandatory requirement for everyone wanting a successful and prosperous life. The inability to control our emotions meant that we were doomed to be controlled by our emotions, and that was a sure path to failure in life. The problem arose when the mindset of keeping our emotions in check started to extend into the emotions arising from grief as a result of a great loss.

It was not until Poppa's death that I realized how difficult it is for so many people to admit that they are grieving. It is as though grief is synonymous with wearing the Scarlet Letter. To grieve in modern-day society is to be shamed and called out for lacking the strength and courage to move on or the faith to stay connected to God. People will say things like "Mama is in a better place," "God knows what's best," and "You can't question God," and all the while, they have a plastered-on fake smile or a face that has aged 30 years overnight due to stress, and they are fighting to stand upright in their dishonesty as the burden of their grief threatens to knock them off their feet onto their knees and finally into a ball of despair and tears. And while those statements may be true, they do not mitigate the excruciating pain the great loss causes one to feel in any way.

Grievers will walk around as imposters pretending like they are 'fine' when they are far from 'fine,' refusing to acknowledge how broken they feel while it is obvious in their demeanor, and passing off their irrational irritability and lightening quick frustration as an issue caused by something someone else did or said.

Grief that is not expressed or acknowledged can have several different presentations.

1. It may show up as the person who is "blessed and highly favored" appearing to have come out on the other end of their great loss unbothered because many Christians are under the false assumption that to grieve is to not believe in God or signifies a lack of faith in God. So many Christians will walk around appearing to have gotten over their great loss while inside, they are hurting and slowly dying. And because they are such great actors and actresses, when the next Christian suffers a great loss, they too pretend to because they received their cue from their fellow sister or brother who also suffered a great loss. That in and of itself is tragic.

2. It may also show up as the person who still maintains their daily routine, appearing to be alive on the outside, but

inside, they are dead, lacking the desire to live, avoiding others, and only forcing themselves to engage in absolutely necessary situations. They stopped living when their loved one stopped living, and they are now merely a shell of the person they used to be. They go to work or school because they must. They try to avoid hanging out with friends and colleagues and have an excuse for not meeting up with them. And if they must hang out, they are just there. They will laugh when they are supposed to, but there is no light in their eyes to match the laughter. They have to remind themselves to eat. And slowly but surely, they try to fade away into the scenery becoming invisible so everyone can leave them alone in their grief.

3. Just as bad is the person doing "the most," as the GenZ's like to say. These are the people living it up! They are out there partying hard, working hard, playing hard, and doing everything in their power to keep their mind occupied. They do not want to have to stop and think about their loss because they know the minute they stop, thoughts of their great loss will swoop in, usurping their ability to ignore the pain. They are working all the time and engaging in all sorts of other activities when they are not working to make sure they are not left with an idle mind that might wander off and start thinking

of their great loss. Because to blissfully ignore the loss feels so much better than having to remember painstakingly.

4. It may show up as the person who is always carrying a spirit of negativity that creates such a strong waste field odor around them that every place they go and every person they meet or encounter is left feeling disgusted due to the nasty stench of grief left behind. They exude nastiness. They are so hurt and in so much pain that they cannot 'fake the funk,' as my mother used to say. They carry their pain on their shoulder like a badge, and if you encounter them, you will surely know their pain because they want you to share in it as well. The saying 'misery loves company' was created for this group. Their grief is so thick all around them that there are no signs of it ever dissipating in the future.

5. And lastly, it may show up as the person appearing to have lost all hope. Their great loss has drained them of all desire, strength, and courage to live. They have difficulty leaving their home. They have trouble interacting with others. They start to miss work or school, creating every excuse possible to explain their absence. They are curled up in their bed, too weak to move, eat, or hope because of their great loss.

They are hoping and praying for God to take them as well and may even have contemplated helping God out. These are the people we especially have to grab hold of and let them know how much they are still loved and needed. Because if we miss how much they are struggling and how severe the pain they are suffering has affected their desire to live, we miss the opportunity to save them from themselves.

Tradition is what makes it impossible for most to break free from the chains of grief that grab hold of many people who suffer a great loss. But freedom from the chains of grief is possible for every one of these people if only they can muster up the strength to fully admit how they are really feeling despite the box that tradition tries to force them into. But it is so hard for so many to admit how they are feeling because of the negative reactions and remarks they are certain to receive from society as a whole, as is the case when anyone dares to admit that they are anything other than strong following a great loss. Where does that come from? When did it start making more sense to pretend not to be affected by a great loss than it is to honestly admit that you are feeling the aftermath of the loss? It is such a disheartening thing that this way of thinking likely originated from cowards who were simply afraid to admit that they felt weak after a great loss, so pretended to be strong and then had the audacity to ridicule anyone else who had the strength and courage to admit that they did feel weak and hurt following a great loss. But history has taught us this one thing repeatedly: it is much easier for people to give in to the ways of society, even the wrong ways of society, rather than go against the grain of society and risk being judged, ridiculed, and gossiped about.

If you get nothing else from this book, please get this… Forget about how society feels about you, your grief, and your emotions. Society has no right to judge how you grieve, when you grieve, nor how long you grieve. It is literally none of their business! Your grief journey can only be properly navigated when you are true to yourself and completely honest and transparent about exactly what you are going through. It is then and only then that you will find freedom and ease in navigating your grief journey. And when you are courageous enough to be honest about your grief, you will find that your path filled with rocky, uneven roads full of potholes of grief will transition to the smoother, asphalt, level roads of recovery.

Experiencing a great loss will cause your world to tilt, your heart to shatter, and your hope to dissipate right before your eyes. And amid all the angst and turmoil running rampant inside, most grievers will still worry about society's traditions and opinions concerning their grief and will expend whatever little energy they have remaining, trying to appear unscathed as though they were anything but grieved. But my question to you is this. Why would anyone want to hide the fact that they are hurting and shattered after a life-changing loss? Do not be a victim of society's opinions and hypocrisy. Do not get trapped in the prison of grief simply because you do not want to admit that you were blessed to have loved and to have been loved and have lost the physical connection to your loved one. You deserve to feel how you feel. Let no one convince you otherwise.

Kimberly Smith Dauterive

Reflections:

Which traditions concerning grief did you unknowingly inherit and have been perpetuating?

How have the traditional ways of handling grief impacted your life? Have they hindered healthy relationships? Caused issues at your place of employment? Hindered your growth as a person or in your career?

Chapter Six: Secret #4 Jesus Grieved

As hard as this may be to believe, tradition is worst of all, in my opinion, amongst Christians. The people who claim to have the strongest belief and most unshakable faith in God are somehow duped into believing that they are above feeling grief. But let me tell you a little secret...even Christians grieve! Just because someone has great faith and just because someone is a born-again Christian who knows the word of God, and goes to church every Sunday or maybe even multiple days of the week does not exempt them from suffering the loss of a loved one because of death. The Bible is very clear that because Adam and Eve sinned, death was sure to come to all of us as a consequence of their disobedience. To think that Christians don't grieve would mean that Christians don't have a heart and don't feel love because at the heart of all of this is the understanding that grief comes from love. To never love even causes grief because of the desire, which is our human nature, to love and to be loved. The act of love is the foundation of Christianity, and therefore, losing something we love will ultimately bring about grief, so Christians are not lucky enough to miss that part of life.

And as long as Christians are not willing to acknowledge that grief, they are highly susceptible to becoming weak and distracted, which inevitably will lead to them being disconnected from God and their purpose. Many times, they are so blinded by their grief that they start to cling to the church, and the pastor becomes their savior because the weight of having ignored their grief is so heavy that they lose their ability to hold on to God. Christians, especially, should feel grief because their love should surpass the love of every other being on this earth, so every time someone or something they love dies, grief should follow. And beware of any Christian who admonishes you for being true to yourself and your grief. They speak from the flesh and not the spirit.

The Bible shows us on more than one occasion that even Jesus grieved. When Lazarus died, Mary and Martha were so distraught that when they saw Jesus, they ran to Him, weeping, saying that if only He had come sooner, their brother would not have died. Now, keep in mind Jesus was returning with the intent to raise Lazarus from the dead so that a miracle could be performed. That was part of His ministry. But even though Jesus knew He was going to raise Lazarus, seeing how distraught Mary and Martha were, the Bible says, He wept. Initially, this really confused me because I thought since He already knew he was going to raise Lazarus from the dead, that it made no sense for Him to be sad about it. But what God laid on my heart one night when I cried out to Him in confusion and despair about my own Poppa's death was that Jesus wasn't weeping because Lazarus died. He was weeping because He felt so grieved and heavy of heart seeing how grieved Mary and Martha were.

Now, let's look at the garden of Gethsemane. Jesus was there praying so hard that He was sweating blood because He knew Judas had betrayed Him and that the crucifixion was near. But Jesus was grieved at having to fulfill that task of the cross, so three times, He asked God to take it away from Him. Three times! Jesus was grieved about what He was about to have to endure. Jesus didn't want to have to go through that pain but knew there was no other way for us to receive salvation and said, "Not my will, but your will be done," to

God in acceptance. So, if Jesus grieved, what makes us think we're so special that we should not?

Do not let any Christian fool you into believing that grieving is sinful. The truth of the matter is people have been taught that to grieve means you don't trust God and that holding onto grief is a sign of one's lack of faith in God. Well, the truth is that grief and faith in God have nothing to do with one another. It is absolutely possible to love something so much that in its absence, you feel heartbroken and sad, and it is also absolutely possible to be broken and sad and still love God and trust God with all your heart. One has nothing to do with the other, in my opinion. You see when my son died, it was the most shattering thing that had ever happened to me in my life. I didn't know up from down, left from right, or night from day. I just simply felt like I was in a perpetual pit of darkness, free falling, and honestly believed that I would never resurface. I was broken and shattered because the inevitability, the finality of death, was made painstakingly clear to me. Not one time did I think God stopped existing because my son wasn't physically here. Not one time did I believe that suddenly, because Poppa was gone from this earth that, God ceased to exist. And not one time did I believe that God's omnipotence and omniscience were anything other than strong and powerful as they had always been. It was during that time that I clung the hardest and tightest to God; who freely gives me grace and mercy I don't deserve each and every day, who has forgiven me over and over again for my many sins, and who loves me in spite of me; because I knew that was the only chance I had of ever surviving.

Grief can only come about when you lose someone or something you love. And for those of us who have been blessed enough to have experienced love, especially those of us who were able to give love and receive love in return, it is unavoidable that at some point, one of us will die. But it's the high cost of the wonderful blessing of love. Because you see the flip side of this is that you could literally go through life and never experience the blessing of love and, therefore, never have to suffer the burden of losing love, but that, in my opinion, is a more horrible existence than the former. To be blessed with love is to know that at some point, you will suffer the loss of that love. So, why is it so hard for people to acknowledge when the loss of a loved one does finally occur, it creates a void so deep within us that, against our will, it gives birth to grief? It's because of the horrible myths, lies, and untruths passed down from generation to generation—the ridiculous traditions. I wonder who the Christian was so many centuries ago who decided that because somebody was grieved about losing a loved one or a pet, or trust after someone's innocence was stolen from them, or betrayal because a fake friend maliciously told your deepest, darkest secrets to someone in any way signified a lack of faith.

One of the most frustrating things that I have come to understand about society is that there are too many people who are willing to just go with the flow, even when the flow is leading them straight over the cliff of a mountain. They follow the ways of tradition without ever questioning them or refuting them. It was a harsh realization for me that there are too many people who refuse to think for themselves. I mean, they literally will take the word of someone else and claim it as gospel without ever looking deeper to verify its truth. They won't investigate it. They won't question the 'why' of it. They'll just say something pitiful like, "That's how it's always been."

Well, I am here to tell you that you do not have to give in to the cowardly ways of society, especially when it comes to grief. I heard a pastor say one time that for every blessing, there is a burden. And the burden of losing a blessing is grief. And if you are courageous enough to go against tradition and acknowledge the grief, it will be the first step you make towards escaping the life-stealing chains that grief has locked on you. Because the truth of the matter is you cannot escape something that you refuse to acknowledge. As long as you refuse to acknowledge the grief and the cause of the grief, it remains evasive and as slippery as soap, and the longer it is not dealt with and not acknowledged, the longer it has to become deeply rooted within you. And deeply rooted grief translates into a life of despair that lacks hope and the ability to ever see the light at the end of the tunnel. My strength came from acknowledging the fact that losing my son hurt like hell!

So, acknowledge it! Don't be afraid to acknowledge it. Don't be afraid to acknowledge something that was extremely important to you and made a huge impact on your life is gone. Don't be afraid to look anyone in the face and say, "I am not doing well." Do not be afraid to acknowledge your grief because others are afraid to acknowledge theirs. Because the longer acknowledgment of grief is avoided, the farther away from getting past it you become. Don't be the reason you can't recover from this grief.

Reflections:

What role has religion played in how you are able to express your grief?

Kimberly Smith Dauterive

Do you believe that having faith in a higher power means you should not grieve?

Escaping the Chains of Grief

What myths about grief have you learned from the church?

Kimberly Smith Dauterive

How have you observed the leaders in your church handle their own grief?

Chapter Seven: Secret #5 It is NOT Good for Grievers to Grieve Alone

As the only child of a single mother, I spent most of my time alone. Now, please don't misunderstand me. I had an amazing mother! We were not rich. Heck, we were not even middle-class, but I never knew that because my mother made sure I had a safe home to live in, a home-cooked meal every night, and everything that I needed, as well as everything that I wanted. But there is a price that comes with those luxuries. You see, because she was a single parent, the only way for me to have those things was for her to go out and work to provide for me. She was an extraordinary provider who was usually gone or on her way out of the door by the time I woke up in the morning and who usually returned home hours after I returned home from school. I was a latchkey kid for quite a while. And because of that, I was usually alone whenever I had to deal with life and the issues that happen in life. So, I had no choice but to learn how to deal with all the ups and downs that went with being an adolescent, preteen, and teenager by myself.

One of the revelations I had as an adult is that we are molded into who we are by all the experiences we've had throughout our lifetime and how we were allowed to express our emotions. Whether we grew to be adults who were able to express our emotions in healthy or unhealthy ways depended upon the methods of expression and freedom of expression we were allowed. This makes me think of the crisis at hand with our teenagers and young adults. My husband used to get so angry when all of the children received an award, whether they won or lost, in a competitive game. He used to say, "There are winners, and there are losers. What's the point of playing if everybody gets the same award?" At the time, I thought it was a good thing to allow all of the kids to feel the joy of receiving something because, in my mind, it was only a game, and as long as they played fair and had fun, they should be rewarded. Boy, has my mindset changed concerning that drastically! It's during our childhood formative years that we are taught essential lessons on how to deal with losses, how to face rejection, and how to control our emotions in the face of disappointments and failures. These are the years when our parents or guardians are supposed to teach us how to win with honor and how to lose with honor. It's the time when temper tantrums happen and give our parents a teaching opportunity to explain to us why it is not appropriate to be upset to the point of self-harm by throwing ourselves on the floor and thrashing about. It's during these years when you might be rejected from a friend group, by a girl or boy you like, by not being chosen to be on the school football, basketball, or volleyball team that you learn how to deal with rejection in an acceptable manner. But because we have failed to allow them to experience these losses and rejections during their childhood when we could have given them the guidance needed to help them manage their raging emotions, we now have adults with adult capabilities, but the emotional and mental capacity of a child. We have done a huge disservice to them all! So, when they inevitably do face losses and rejection, we see the temper tantrums manifested as shootings, disregard for authority, and lack of respect for everyone, including themselves. Learning how to express emotions properly is a vital part of our childhood. And it's something we're going to have to return to if we expect to survive the next 50 years or so.

But I digress, back to the matter at hand. Because I was always alone, I learned how to deal with every situation by myself. So, if I had a problem with friends being messy or betraying me, I dealt with the hurt and confusion on my own. If my little kiddie love relationship fell apart, I dealt with the heartbreak on my own. If I was feeling gloomy, sad, awkward, or misunderstood, I just simply learned how to smother those emotions until they eventually passed, so again, I figured out how to deal with those emotions on my own. And because I have always dealt with conflict and losses on my own since my childhood, it's not surprising that I grew up to be an adult who continued to deal with my problems in the same manner.

During times of conflict, chaos, loss, or any disturbance to the normalcy of my life, alone is where I am most comfortable. To have people try to come in and fix things for me or try to give me unsolicited advice are some of the most uncomfortable situations I've ever been put in. Regardless of whether the intention is pure or not, because I have been molded over the course of 36 years to handle every experience in that fashion, it was not a mold that would be easily broken. When I got married at the age of 36, it took a lot of time and work on my part to learn that our union as husband and wife also meant that I had to share my thoughts and my strategies for dealing with issues as they came about. My husband, who happens to come from the classic American household (mom, dad, and sister), was accustomed to having his family involved in his problems as they arose. That was a huge problem for me! I believe the cause of the first real argument we had was him bringing OUR problem to his family to solve. But I've learned over the years that problem-solving by myself in our marriage was only going to serve to weaken our marriage ultimately.

Guess where else problem-solving alone does not work? When it comes to grief! After Poppa died, I literally wanted to disappear and go to a place where nobody knew me, where I could process this horrific ordeal on my own. Because my husband was severely injured in the crash, we literally had people in and out of our home all day, every day. And that drove me nuts! You see, at this point, I had spent 36 years of my life processing losses and dealing with grief by myself and had only spent twelve years of my life being married to my husband and dealing with things in union with him. So, when the most shattering and crushing experience of my life occurred, and my husband wasn't able to help me process this traumatizing loss in a healthy manner, I naturally reverted back to the natural habit of protecting myself that was deeply imprinted within my core, to grieve alone.

I didn't want visitors. I didn't want to go anywhere. I didn't want to hear the traditional words and phrases, which were like daggers in my heart. I didn't want to be bothered with people who were coming around but were never in my inner circle. Now, the thing about losing a loved one is that the community as a whole wants to show up and let you know that they are there for you, which is noble and honorable. However, when you're going through a life experience that feels like you're caught in the eye of a tornado, you don't really want the unfamiliar around. At least, that's the case for me and people like me. Having to deal with unfamiliar people during those moments makes already unstable emotions spin wildly out of control. The issue is that the community doesn't know your quirks or your qualms. They don't know you don't like unexpected visitors. They don't know you're exhausted from being up crying all night and are just not in the mood to entertain company just by looking at you. They don't know that you're one "You can't question God" away from body-slamming them on the ground. Your tribe knows! And they know because they're familiar with subtle changes in your voice and your demeanor. But the community doesn't know. While they are truly just trying to be helpful, the reality is that they are sometimes causing more harm.

I have to admit, it's difficult enough trying to manage what is usual. So, trying to manage the unusual was almost too much for me to bear. And expressing my emotions was a completely different ordeal. My tribe knew to be present, but to allow me the space I needed to process everything. They helped where help was needed. They took tasks away from me that they knew I would not willingly give up because it's hard for me to ask for help. They were there to let me cry on their shoulder, to lift my spirit with movies and happy memories, and to pull me out of the pit of hell when I started sliding quickly downward toward it with my unhealthy thoughts. They knew to be ears for listening, arms for doing, and hands for helping, not mouths for saying empty phrases. But the community, on the other hand, wanted to come in and say the magic words that were supposed to help me to feel better, not realizing because of tradition that those magic words weren't magic words at all, but daggers piercing my heart every time they were spoken, snuffing out the fire of the last bit of hope that may have still been burning in me. And that's a huge reason behind the isolation that is desired by a lot of grievers. Grievers will try and stay in isolation to protect themselves from those encounters. So, grievers will resort to crying in the privacy of their rooms, their bathrooms, their closets, and even in their cars just to avoid the meaningless and harmful words traditionally spoken by most of society. It's difficult enough trying to process the horrible events that have occurred in your life but trying to process those emotions while trying not to be triggered or offended by people who are just trying to help is too much for any griever to try and juggle around. Most likely, the juggling will be tragically unsuccessful, and either the griever will be further wounded or the supporter will leave with a new wound of their own.

But there is a huge problem with grievers grieving alone. In isolation, grievers are left to battle the onslaught of negative mindsets and crippling thoughts that emerge from out of nowhere. And the longer they grieve or are left alone with their thoughts, the more they will find themselves free-falling through the deep, dark hole of the abyss with no one there to pull them out. Isolation makes you unknowingly put yourself in danger of being attacked in your most vulnerable state by the evil that is always lurking around us. The devil is busy trying to gain souls every second of the day, and it is when you are isolated, weakened by your grief, that he attacks the hardest and the most relentlessly.

So, to every griever out there, listen closely.

I see you hiding in the corner over there. I see you trying to hide your tears. I see you trying to isolate yourself because it's the only time you don't have to pretend to be strong when you're really not. I see you crying in the shower, in your closet, in the laundry room, and in your car. I see you!! And I need for you to know this… IT IS O. K.

It's okay to express your hurt in the company of your family and friends. It's okay to show your pain amongst your coworkers. It's okay to cry in front of your children. But it's NOT okay to hide or bury those painful emotions that are fighting to get out of you and be expressed. Because the longer those emotions are allowed to fester inside unexpressed, the more they are able to distance you from all the people still here that you love and care about.

And that's the real objective of the devil in the first place, isn't it? The devil is using the loss of your physical connection with one of your precious loved ones to trick you into becoming emotionally distanced and disconnected from your other precious loved ones who are still here.

The devil will try to consume you with that one loss so much that it literally blinds you to the many things you still have. And how does he do it? He isolates you! He sends people to make you feel uncomfortable or embarrassed about crying in front of them. Or people who want to give you advice about an experience that they have no idea about because they've never dealt with it before. And he'll even send people who think they're comforting you to say things like "he's in a better place" when those words are like knives stabbing you over and over. And he does this to grieve your heart so much that you don't want to be around anyone! So you isolate yourself.

And the truth of the matter is that the worst place for a griever to be is alone. Don't fall into his trap.

The Bible tells us that he is the great deceiver. It's in those moments of isolation that the devil sneaks in and starts whispering all sorts of lies in your ear.

Lies like...

You won't survive this.

You don't deserve to be happy.

You're too weak to live with purpose.

You see, the devil knows it's easy to convince you to believe his lies when you're hurting and alone. That's why the devil tries to keep you isolated! He knows that if your tribe is there surrounding you and supporting you, as soon as he starts with the lies, they will step in and remind you of all you still have and who God made you to be.

In Ecclesiastes Chapter 4, verses 9 through 12, the Bible says, "Two are better than one, If either of them falls down, one can help the other up... Though one may be overpowered, two can defend themselves".

So don't hide! Don't be ashamed of your grief. Never be afraid to express your emotions, especially when you are expressing emotions concerning someone God blessed you to love and be loved by.

This is your grief journey to travel, and no one has the right to tell you how to navigate this rough and rocky road. You have a right to feel how you feel, whenever you feel that way, wherever you feel it, and for however long the emotion lasts. And nobody, and I do mean nobody, has the right to tell you otherwise. Don't isolate yourself and give the devil the advantage. Surround yourself with your tribe, the people who love you and will help you to ignore the lies and remember all the blessings that you still have.

That Ecclesiastes verse ends by saying,

"A cord of three strands is not quickly broken." that's you, your tribe, and God.

Reflections:

Are you more comfortable grieving alone, or do you allow your family and friends to support you in your grief? Why?

Can you recall the ways that you have been attacked (how negative thoughts tried to convince you of untruths) while you were grieving alone?

Escaping the Chains of Grief

How have your family & friends been able to rescue you from the path of negative thoughts you were headed down?

Chapter Eight: Secret #6 Time Is Not a Healer of a Broken Heart

As an internist who has been practicing for over 20 years, I have probably seen cases of almost every bone in the body broken. And I've witnessed those bones go through their healing stages until they were all mended back together again. I've seen people with broken tibias or fibulas, and even both at times, who were initially unable to walk progressively improve to the point where they gradually transitioned from using crutches then to an orthotic boot until finally, they graduated to walking again on their own unassisted. I've also managed patients who had strokes and suffered brain damage, which left them paralyzed on one side of their body, who were able to regain some, and in a few cases all, of the function of their limbs with the help of physical therapy. I've even treated patients who've had heart attacks and watched them go from barely being able to walk a few feet to running miles a day. But the notion that time can heal a heart that is broken because someone or something they love has died... now that is just unfathomable.

There is a medical disorder called Takotsubo syndrome; in Layman's terms, it stands for Broken Heart Syndrome. The disorder was discovered when doctors realized that following the death of a spouse, for those who had been married for four or more decades, it was very common that the death of the surviving spouse was soon to follow. And while the first spouse's death was likely due to an actual medical issue, the surviving spouse's death was usually the result of grief. When I did some research to understand Broken Heart Syndrome better, I learned that the issue at hand had to do with substances called neurotransmitters, which are supposed to be beneficial and protective for us but which, when elevated for prolonged periods of time, are detrimental. These are the neurotransmitters responsible for our "fight or flight" response as part of our Sympathetic Nervous System. These neurotransmitters are supposed to be elevated for short periods during times of grief and stress in order to increase our heart rate, dilate our blood vessels, and provide extra blood and oxygen to our organs, especially our muscles, so that we can respond properly to sudden stressors in our lives, such as a dog attack. During those short periods, the elevated neurotransmitters benefit our health and wellness. However, when these same neurotransmitters are elevated continuously for prolonged periods of time because of grief and constant stress, they become detrimental and could actually lead to the heart becoming weakened to the point of performing at only 10% to 15% of its norm.

Thinking about Takutsubo Syndrome and knowing how devastated I felt after Poppa's death and the length of time that nasty emotion lingered gives me the clarity to understand how such a syndrome exists. My heart has ached every single day for the past four years. I don't know how I avoided the syndrome, and all I can say is, "Thank you, God, for covering me." The realization that there's a piece of my heart missing that Poppa's presence used to fill, which is now empty, has led me to learn the third secret to escaping the jaws of grief. Time really won't heal my broken heart.

When you lose someone you love, it's almost comical that anyone can truly believe that time is going to heal that wound.

As I mentioned, it's been four years since Poppa went to Paradise, and I still wake up every morning praying it was all a bad dream. Unfortunately, every morning when I open my eyes, I'm hit with the reality that he's really gone. And because of that, sadness has become my new norm. People say, "Time heals." however, I have a hard time believing that one morning in 5, 10, or even 20 years, I will wake up and not feel sad that my baby boy is not physically here for me to hug and kiss and love on him. You see, that's the thing. Being physically disconnected from someone you love is what causes the grief in the first place. So, unless that physical connection is restored, how then can the sadness go away?

Now, let's delve more into grief and sadness. I believe these two emotions are two different types of emotions. Sadness is the emotion that I feel because I cannot see, hear, or feel my baby boy. But grief, on the other hand, is the unexpressed emotion I feel that I have yet to acknowledge and deal with. Until those emotions are fully and honestly expressed, the grief will always linger. And I believe that it's grief, which is the ultimate culprit, that leads to broken heart syndrome.

So, tell me, how could I ever get over it? I mean, just think about it. The only logical way to repair this level of brokenness is by bringing Poppa back, and since that was not and still is not an option, then there is no mending this broken heart. And don't get me started on how I foolishly believed the lie that "time heals all wounds." That's one of the biggest lies of them all. Every morning when I wake up, I am slapped in the face with the hardcore truth that I am not dreaming and that my baby boy is gone. So, you see, when I say there will always be an undercurrent of sadness within my soul for the rest of my life, that's why! For basically every human being, the loss of their loved one will cause their heart to break, and when that heart, like Humpty Dumpty, is put back together again, there is usually a piece missing. A vital piece missing! Considering that the heart is one of the major organs your body needs to survive, that is not mediocre. So, stop telling people, "Time will heal, " because it's not true! The sooner a griever can understand and come to terms with that, the sooner relief from the pain of grief may come. To be told to believe in something that is just not true or something that will never come to pass is cruel. And again, while people are only trying to be helpful, we need to be more truthful about how those traditional phrases harm instead of help. The loss of a loved one is already one of the most difficult times any person will ever have to go through. Let's not make it any harder with traditional words and phrases that are merely myths and hold not one ounce of truth within them.

While time will not heal my broken heart, I have come to a place where I've learned to live with my new normal. You see, I realized that I will be sad every day because my baby boy is not here. And I don't even wish not to feel the sadness because to do so would also mean that I had forgotten him. It's no different from having your child move across the world to a place where you cannot physically connect with him. Imagine a time before cell phones, FaceTime, Zoom, or any technology readily available today. If you were separated from your loved one by an ocean and had no way to talk to them or, love on them, or even to simply say, "I love you", imagine how devastating that would be for you and how grieved you would be. That is how death functions and how grief is so easily able to consume the lives of everyone who has to deal with it. But if we can get to a place where we can acknowledge the fact that the sadness will always be there as long as our loved one is physically disconnected from us, then we prevent grief from digging its roots deep within our souls and robbing us of the rest of our lives. Don't forget, this is all about surviving grief! Surviving grief means acknowledging the lies and the myths and embracing the truth so that we can have freedom from the grief that has had us in bondage without hope.

Reflections:

Have you been deceived into believing that time is going to heal the pain from losing someone or something you love?

How did you handle it?

Kimberly Smith Dauterive

When did you lose your loved one, and how has time affected your emotions overall?

Escaping the Chains of Grief

What has happened to you over time as a result of losing a loved one? Are you emotionally present for your loved ones still here? Are you living with purpose or just existing?

Chapter Nine: SECRET #7 Moving Forward Doesn't Mean Forgetting Your Loved One

The first Halloween following Poppa's death, our house stayed shut up in the dark. I just could not convince myself to participate in any of the Trick-or-Treating or to enjoy the costumes of the little ones because it was just too painful. I remember leaving my office after work and seeing some of the kids in their costumes excitedly running up to houses in search of the coveted Halloween candy and my heart instantly felt like a ton of bricks was dropped on it. "What would Poppa have dressed up as this year?" The question kept scrolling through my thoughts over and over again because Halloween was a big deal for him.

When Thanksgiving rolled around, I knew I wasn't going to participate in that either. My heart was too heavy. How could I even think about celebrating the holidays without

Poppa? At the time, I couldn't even take into consideration how our other kids felt. It worked out well enough because, as a blended family, the younger kids were with their mother, my oldest son was in another country on active duty with the Army, and my daughter didn't care because she would have spent most of her time in her room anyway as is the case for most teenagers of the GenZ era. I couldn't fathom trying to enjoy the company of our family as we would normally do. Not without Poppa, whose absence was like the largest sinkhole that appeared out of nowhere, consuming everything and everyone in its vicinity. As a matter of fact, we were only able to eat a proper Thanksgiving dinner because our family brought us some food despite our objections, for which we were very grateful.

By the time Christmas rolled around, I felt as though I was dragging a 2-ton heart around. Every decoration, every Christmas song, and every commercial showing a Christmas sale brought pain and agony to my heart. This holiday was proving to be the most difficult of all to endure. It was just too much to handle. Thinking about not getting that welcomed disruption of my sleep on Christmas morning by an excited Poppa who would undoubtedly be beyond ready to open his gifts was tearing me apart inside. So, we ran. We left our home; we left the state and rode out the holiday at a hotel where we could be alone in our misery and cry our hearts out. We had to escape the love and support our family and friends, without a doubt, would pour out on us because, despite their good intentions, it was all too much to deal with. All I wanted to do was curl up in the fetal position, cover my head with a blanket and bawl until the painful burden that was crushing my heart eased up a bit. And when that pain would build up again, I would cry again. It's hard to do that with people around because instinctively, they want to do something or say something to make you feel better, but interceding with hugs and words during those times only felt like sharp jabs to my already wounded soul. Now, please don't misunderstand me. I love my tribe. I would not have made it without them. But at that time, with the wound so fresh still, I just wanted to curl up in the fetal position with the blanket covering even my head and cry the ugliest cry possible. I didn't want to feel obligated to get out of bed, eat, or even shower. I just wanted to be left alone.

The problem with the holidays, especially the first two years after Poppa's death, was that it just did not seem right to celebrate without him. And if I'm being perfectly transparent, it still doesn't feel quite right. In those first two years, I couldn't see or think beyond my grief, and the thought of celebrating anything without Poppa caused a piercing pain inside of me. So, we didn't celebrate any holidays. When my husband and I built our home, we built it with the absolute intention of hosting all, or at least the majority, of our family gatherings. Poppa's death put a huge boulder in the way of our holiday celebrations as a family because I felt that our family was no longer complete. I knew the rest of our family deserved to still have us present for them and that it wasn't fair for them to be deprived of the holidays and making new memories with us. Still, grief had me in a chokehold so tight that I could barely breathe, so I honestly could not muster up the strength to even fight it.

The first year was horrible, of course. We pretty much did not expect to be participating in any festivities. We did not go on our usual yearly family vacation. We did not celebrate any of the holidays. We did, however, celebrate Poppa though. When his birthday rolled around, we got a cake and sang "Happy Birthday" to him. On the anniversary of his first year in Paradise, we even had a beautiful balloon release in memory of him. It was amazing because people who loved Poppa from all over went live on Facebook with their balloons and paid homage to our Poppa Bear with their tributes. It was painful and wonderful at the same time. And when the second year rolled around, I started breathing a bit easier because surely, year two would be better than year one. Boy, was I wrong! I can honestly say that I believe the second year was worse simply because I expected to feel better. So, when the holidays rolled around, and I found myself again in the fetal position, crying my eyes out, feeling like my heart was breaking all over again, I was truly surprised and discouraged. When was this going to end? I mean, was that really going to be my life forever?

In year number three, my daughter came to me and said that she had spoken with one of her classmates who had participated in a program that walks people who are grieving through the steps to recovering from the grief and that it sounded like something she would like to do. And so, we did it as a family in support of her. This was such a huge blessing to me. This program changed my life forever as a griever! Over the course of 7 weeks, I was able to dig through my pain, discover the reason behind my method of grieving and dealing with such a huge loss, and break free from the hold that grief had on me that was keeping me stagnant and unable to move. This program helped me reach a place where I felt I could move forward. What I realized is that a lot of my hesitancy with moving forward was that I was under the misconceived notion that shedding off my grief meant that I was trying to shed off my memories of Poppa. And that couldn't be further from the truth. This program helped me to recognize the seventh secret to escaping the chains of grief: moving forward does not mean forgetting about your loved ones.

I believe that so many people hold on to their grief and suffering because it's their way of holding on to their loved one's memories. To move on or move forward and enjoy life to many seems as though they are leaving their loved ones behind and forgetting about them and their importance in their lives. It makes perfect sense now why, 30 or 40 years after a loved one's death, people will still be so grieved and not able to move forward. Their grief has them anchored to the loss of their loved one, and that anchor has kept them so stagnant in their personal growth that grief has been allowed to dig deep roots within their soul and has taken control of their ability to live and have a purpose.

So many people are under the misguided notion that moving forward and living after the death of their loved one means that they are choosing to forget their loved one, almost as though they fell out of love with them. But that is the farthest thing from the truth. I realized that the more I talked about Poppa and told his story, the more I kept his spirit alive. The more I regained my strength and regained control of my emotions, which had been running haywire, unleashed, and unmanaged, the more I could live again. You see, I recognized that the devil wants us stuck in the past anchored to our loss so that we are not present in the lives of the people who are still here with us. The devil keeps us focused on the one loss and has us ignoring the others who are still here all around us and who continue to deserve our love as well. But grief will blind us to the point that we can't even see what we still have because we are so focused on the loss. And that in and of itself is a tragedy.

By Thanksgiving, number three, I lie in my bed and suddenly thought about my daughter who had always been very shy, which was one of the motivating factors for why we always had family gatherings at our home. She has always felt most comfortable at our own home where she grew up and could more easily interact with family members on her own terms at her own pace without feeling out of place. That arrangement allowed her to foster bonds with family members without the threat of feeling emotionally overloaded and not having her own space to retreat to. She could retreat to her room until she felt better. As I lay in my bed on Thanksgiving of 2021, God spoke clearly to me and said if you don't start integrating with the family again, neither will she, and if something happens to you, she'll be alone because you're not giving her the opportunity now to overcome her shyness and her trepidation with being in larger crowds. Now that got my attention! Because the last thing in the world that I wanted my grief to do was hinder the growth of my children, who are still here. So that got my mind right and from that moment on, we started working our way back into our family's lives and being present at more family gatherings. We even hosted Christmas that year and had a wonderful time.

Living and enjoying life by no means indicates that you're forgetting about your loved one. As a matter of fact, we talk about Poppa so much now at every family gathering and in our everyday lives that you would swear he is still here. Another secret I found is that the more I talk about him, the stronger his spirit seems to be around me. And that is worth me talking about him 24 hours a day, seven days a week! Moving forward doesn't mean that you forget about your loved one. It simply means that you continue to live the life that you were created to live. I am a firm believer that God has each and every one of us here for an implicit purpose. If we allow the death of our loved ones to burden us and grieve us so much that we stop living and start just existing, then we will never be able to fulfill the purpose for which we were created. And if we stay curled up in bed, or become mummified because of our loss, or if we don't live up to our full potential, then our loved one's memories will really die. You see, the grief merely keeps us anchored to the loss and keeps the memory of our loved ones imprisoned in our minds and our hearts but not in the atmosphere of the community. I did not want Poppa's memory to be strongly embedded within the recesses of just my mind; I wanted everybody to remember him. And I'm sure you feel the same way about your loved one. But you can't keep their memory alive if grief has you so anchored to the time that they were taken away from you that you can barely speak about your loved one without being overwhelmed with tears.

So, if you truly want to hold on to the memories of your

loved one, if you truly want to keep their spirit and legacy alive, you have to live. And the only way for you to live is for you to keep moving forward with purpose. And I do not care if you have to drag yourself, limp, or crawl; just do not stop moving! You owe it to your loved one to live and fulfill your purpose and to keep their legacy and their memory alive. It's up to you to determine whether or not you are going to let grief win. Will you let their memory die out and fade away as you die out and fade away, or will you keep their memory strong in the community and in the minds of everyone who knew your loved one as well? Will you keep growing in strength and resilience and allow your loved one's memory to grow as well? The choice is yours, but keep in mind that you can build nothing if you are not living. And just like everything else in your life will fade away if you allow yourself to fade away, so will the memory of your loved one. And that alone, in my opinion, is worth fighting for. So, get up, put your shoes, on and get dressed. Fight for you and fight for your loved one's memory. Because they deserve it, and so do you.

Kimberly Smith Dauterive

Reflections:

Have you been unintentionally neglecting the loved ones still here by focusing on the one who isn't?

What have you been doing to avoid dealing with the pain that shows up with grief?

Escaping the Chains of Grief

Do you have a different perspective now about keeping your loved one's memory alive?

Chapter Ten: Live Life With Purpose On Purpose

I think Forrest Gump said it best, "Life is like a box of chocolates. You never know what you're gonna get." Life is truly like that...full of surprises, full of ups, full of downs. Full of curveballs is maybe the best way to put it. I've had many beautiful moments and achievements throughout my life. I graduated salutatorian of my high school class. I graduated from the best college in my state. I became a very successful Internal Medicine physician. I have a beautiful family and so many more things that I am grateful for. But I have also had many bad moments that rival the good. I have suffered through an abusive relationship as a young, confused, and afraid teenager, being alone most of the time as a latchkey kid, being betrayed, being deceived, being lied to, being cheated on, having a pregnancy complication that caused me to lose a child, and losing my mother to cancer. But nothing, and I do mean not a single thing I have ever been through in my life, brought me to my knees and the brink of insanity like the unexpected, tragic death of my 9-year-old son, Poppa. Despite all the trauma and pain that I have had to endure, though, my faith has never wavered.

When I was 12 years old, I remember praying the prayer of salvation while in my aunt's living room led by Bishop Jeffery Archangel. That was a very memorable moment in my life. You see, God has had His hand on my life ever since I was a little girl. I was drawn to Him at an early age after receiving my first Bible from my mother when I was about ten years old. I was captivated by the stories and felt more drawn to God as I read them repeatedly.

Nevertheless, trials and tribulations still came my way. And it's almost as though the devil really had an issue with my relationship with God because it seemed as though he threw everything he had at me. It didn't matter though. While the winds whipped fiercely and the thunderstorms tried hard to break me down, I may have bent horribly here and there, and I may have even stumbled and fallen from time to time. Nevertheless, the relationship that I had already nurtured with

Father God has kept me from breaking completely. You see, in my mind, as a daughter of the most high God, I believe with every fiber of my being that "all things work together for the good of those who love the Lord (Romans 8:28)." And "all things" means good things and bad things. So, when bad things have happened to me, I have never freaked out or given in to the pity party of "woe is me" because that relationship I nurtured through the years has developed within me unshakable faith. I actually do believe that if God allowed it to happen, he allowed it to happen for a reason. And that had always been good enough for me.

But when Poppa died, it was the first time I had ever felt broken. My faith never changed. I still believed in God and His Word, and I still do believe today. But one of the most surprising epiphanies I had during my grief journey is that my pain, my sadness, my brokenness caused by the destruction of the physical connection I had to Poppa has nothing at all to do with my faith in God. I will never understand how those two things became synonymous in most Christians' minds.

The Bible is clear in its statement that all of our days are numbered. So, it is irrefutable that one day, we will all die. And that also means we will all have to suffer through losing someone we love at some point in our lives. Before Poppa's death, I never understood why people would be so grieved when their loved one died because, in my naive mind, the endgame was always Heaven. I am not saying I did not understand why people were sad. Of course, I expected people to feel sad and hurt when someone they love died. What I did not understand was the grief that held them in bondage, the grief that stopped them from living. If we believe in God and believe that Heaven is real, then why wouldn't we be sad that our loved one is gone and rejoice that they finally were called up to Paradise? Well, Poppa's death cleared up most of my confusion.

Regardless of all the bad things that have happened in my life, I have maintained my unwavering resolve, faith, and trust in God. But the devil found a small crack in my fort that he managed to squeeze through without issue and used it to bring me down to my knees, to a level of brokenness I was so unfamiliar with that I did not believe I would survive. I did not want to be here. Now, I have never contemplated suicide, but I have told my family over and over again that if something happens to me, I am ill or extremely hurt, or on my deathbed, they are not to pray for me to be healed or for me to stay here on this earth because I want to go and be with my baby boy, my Poppa Bear. I don't perceive it as selfish either because I feel that my loved ones here will still have each other even if I am not here. But as a mother, I cannot shake the feeling that my Poppa is in Heaven all by himself and that I should be there with him. A good mother never stops worrying about her children. Even when they are grown, a mother worries, so to not be able to lay eyes or hands on your children is torture.

Nevertheless, I am here. And if I am here, that means the Lord still has a purpose for my life. We are not meant to be here just to exist. God created each and every one of us for a specific purpose, and it is our job to figure out that purpose based on our natural inclinations, talents, and abilities and to fulfill that purpose. Looking back at Poppa's funeral, I can still see that our church, which seats over 900 people, was Standing Room Only. For the entire viewing hours, the line was so long that it stretched beyond the sanctuary's doors to the outside where people waited patiently to get inside so that they could pay their last respects to Poppa and give my husband and me their condolences. There were so many people that, unfortunately, everyone did not get the opportunity to get in even though the doors of the church opened at 7 am and the funeral did not start until 11 am. The doors had to be closed so the funeral could begin, and some people could not get in. That is how huge an impact Poppa and his great big personality and his knack for loving people unconditionally had on the entire community, no scratch that, the entire region. That is what living life with purpose on purpose truly looks like.

One of the pastors, Pastor Eric Fondal, said something that really struck a chord in my heart and has stayed with me ever since. He said that Poppa lived his life in "fortissimo." Fortissimo is a musical term that describes playing at a high, full-volume level. But playing at that level is meant to be done for only a short period of time. So, for nine years, I can attest that Poppa lived his life in fortissimo until finally, God gave him his rest. I can promise you that he did not waste a single day in fulfilling his purpose. He made everyone, young and old, rich and poor, black and white feel good about themselves, feel included, and feel loved. Even when we went on vacation, Poppa always found a stranger to make into a friend, and he always found an older person of all races to sit and engross in conversation that was evidently so good that the older persons usually did not want the conversation to end. It was like that everywhere we went. He made everyone he encountered feel special. And I am still today, four years later, hearing stories of how Poppa made a difference in someone's life. I believe that every single one of us has a purpose similar to Poppa's that is meant to impact the lives of people both near and far, young and old, just like Poppa did.

Think about the numerous lives impacted because of the love and kindness that Poppa showed every chance he could. Think about the number of additional lives that will be impacted by all of the people whose lives were directly impacted by Poppa. Now…think about the tens of thousands or the hundreds of thousands of lives that Poppa has impacted either directly or indirectly. THAT is what fulfilling our purpose should look like!

So, let's reflect and have a good old come to Jesus moment now. If we stay stuck in our grief and do not fulfill our purpose, how many lives will we fail to impact? How many people will never reach their full potential because we stopped living and started existing because we let grief win? How many hundreds of thousands of people's lives will not be transformed because we refuse to fight and sever the ties to the anchor that keeps us stuck in the past with our grief?

We were not created to sit back and succumb to the painful emotions that grief happily loves to hand out to everyone in its path. We were not created to only live for and build the lives of ourselves and our own families. We were not designed to be selfish nor to keep our unique qualities and extraordinary skills to ourselves that we were innately born with and supposed to share with others for the successful evolution of mankind. No! We were created for a purpose, which is not just for us but for impacting other people's lives on monumental levels. When I look at all the things I've been through in my life, I know that all those experiences, especially the bad ones, have molded me into the resilient, confident, courageous, brave, wise, and extraordinary woman I am today. Without those experiences, I would not be any of those things. I would not be me, and neither would you be you. Knowing that we have been born to fulfill specific purposes at specific times in our lives, I want to challenge you to refuse to give in to the temptation to curl up in a ball under your blankets and just stay there and cry. Refuse to allow grief to consume every part of your being until it bubbles over and, as collateral damage, affects your loving relationships with the people you still have present here on earth who love you and care about you. Refuse to allow grief to rob you of your life, your life's purpose, and your ability to impact the lives you were meant to transform so that they can live to reach their highest potential and have a chance to live life with purpose on purpose. Our lives are not just for us. And just as everything that we do has an impact on people, so does everything that we do not do.

Who are you holding back because you're stuck? Whose life will never be impacted because you decided to give up? How many lives will never be transformed because you decided to let grief win? And I hate to be the bearer of bad news, but the ugly truth is this: staying stuck in your grief is a choice. I know it doesn't feel that way. I know it seems like you just don't have the strength or the courage to get up and overcome it. And I know you have seen grief win the battle in so many other people's lives, but that does not mean it will be the same for your life. Remember Goliath? Everyone was afraid, and no one wanted to fight him because he was so large and had already defeated so many before them. But David did not care about how things had gone before he got there. All David knew was that God had victoriously gotten him through every battle he had fought in his past, and he had no doubt that

God would show up again and give him victory over Goliath. And God did!! So, ignore what people have said and done as slaves to tradition and society and remember the many situations God has gotten you through, which I am sure are too many to count, in your past, and trust that if He did it before, He will most definitely do it again. But you have to do your part: keep your focus on God, trust His process, and know that no matter what it looks like or feels like in real-time, in the end, you will overcome that horrible grief.

So, choose to drag yourself out of that bed. Choose to ignore the lies the devil is shouting in your ears throughout the day. Choose to rely on God's strength to get you through each and every day. Choose to believe that though grief may have won a battle, it will not win the war. Choose to live and not just exist. The choice is yours. The easy route is to just give up, but you owe it to yourself, your children, your legacy, and the memory of your loved ones to fight to fulfill your purpose in this life.

So, fight alongside me and make a conscious decision to stay in the fight until we have reclaimed the power taken from us by grief. We deserve to live in peace. We deserve to still have joy and happiness even though there will always be an undercurrent of grief lingering because we will never stop missing our loved ones. And above all else, we deserve to thrive, soar, and do what God created us to do: LIVE LIFE WITH PURPOSE ON PURPOSE.

Reflections:

Are you living your life with purpose?

Kimberly Smith Dauterive

How are you impacting the lives of the people around you?

Escaping the Chains of Grief

Whose life may never be changed for the better if you don't fight to fulfill your purpose?

Acknowledgments

I never thought I'd ever write a book but there are people out there who knew I had a book in me, actually several books, and kept pushing me until I finally started writing. If it weren't for them, I would have never survived the loss of my son and I would have never found the courage nor the voice that allows me to transform lives the way I'm able to do so now.

To my husband, Phillip, thank you so much for your constant encouragement and for never missing the opportunity to remind me of how strong and impactful I am and how much my story needs to be heard by others. Thank you for pushing me to be the best version of myself that God intended for me to be.

To my children J. J. and Leah, you are my heart beats that keep me going and my love for you is one of my greatest inspirations. Thank you for helping me to connect with the social media world to get my brand recognized. Your love for me and mine for you is what picks up the slack in the part of my heart that's injured and lagging because of Poppa's absence. Thank you for loving me and lifting me up and motivating me to keep putting one foot in front of the other.

Thank you to my Savoy family and my JKL family for your constant support and encouragement, especially my cousin Paula and Ms. Celestine, who have been pushing me to write this book for quite a while, my aunt Charlotte and cousin Rod for not allowing me to vanish in my pain but enhanced our connections so I would stay present, and Janaia, Latasha, and Tawanna for loving on me and keeping JKL running smoothly through my storm.

Thank you, Tawanna, for literally forcing a pen into my hand and creating platforms for me to start writing. And for making it so easy for me with your beautiful creations to share my story through writing, blogging, social media, and everything else you've done because it's so much. You are the best.

Thank you to my Tribe (Dana, Malik, Lucretia, Rori, Anika, and Tawanna) that God allows me to do life with. You ladies are all phenomenal. My family and I survived the worst event in our lives because of you. Your support, insight, and advice as I've gone through this process means everything.

And if I have forgotten anyone, please charge it to my head and not my heart! So many, along the way, have encouraged and motivated me as I embarked upon this new journey. Please know that I am appreciative of each and every one of you and if I missed you for this book, I promise I won't for the next. Because there will be a next!

About the Author

Dr. Kimberly Smith Dauterive is a Board-Certified Internal Medicine Physician. She was born in Washington D.C. but grew up in St. Martinville, LA. She was raised as an only child by her phenomenal mother, Lorraine Savoy, in a single parent household where she learned how to be strong despite the obstacles, courageously independent, and how to boldly live life with purpose.

Dr. Kim graduated as salutatorian of her class in 1989 from St. Martinville Senior High School in St. Martinville, LA then went on to receive her Bachelor of Science Degree in 1993 from Tulane University in New Orleans, LA; her Master of Science Degree in 1996 from the University of Southwestern Louisiana in Lafayette, LA (now the University of Louisiana at Lafayette); and her Doctor of Medicine Degree in 2000 from Louisiana State University Health Sciences Center in New Orleans, LA.

She is the owner of JKL Healthcare Services, a private medical practice located in New Iberia LA, and provides exemplary personalized healthcare to her patients using both allopathic and holistic medicine to meet her patient's needs.

Her motto is that total patient care means "healing the mind, body, and spirit". She is the co-owner of Total Health and Wellness and PKD Housing Rentals, LLC, and co-founder of the Phillip Poppa Dauterive III Foundation created in honor of her 9-year-old son who was tragically taken from her and her family. Turning her pain into purpose, Dr. Kim became a certified Advanced Grief Recovery Method Specialist and created the DoctorKSD Evolved Brand to help others by empowering them with the proper tools to navigate life after any type of the loss, to reprogram their mindsets, and to see themselves as the amazing creations they were designed to be through her P.A.V.E. The Way and Mold Me programs.

Dr. Kim has shared a life-bond with Phillip Dauterive, whom she's been blissfully married to since 2007. She is the mother of James, Leah, 2 Angels now residing in Heaven- Phillip III "Poppa" and Mallory, and 4 bonus children. Dr. Smith is also a transformer, motivator, nurturer, and a woman of God. She loves being an advocate for the well-being of her family, her patients, and her community and strives to fulfill her mission statement of "healing the mind, body and spirit" and empowering others to "Live Life With Purpose On Purpose".